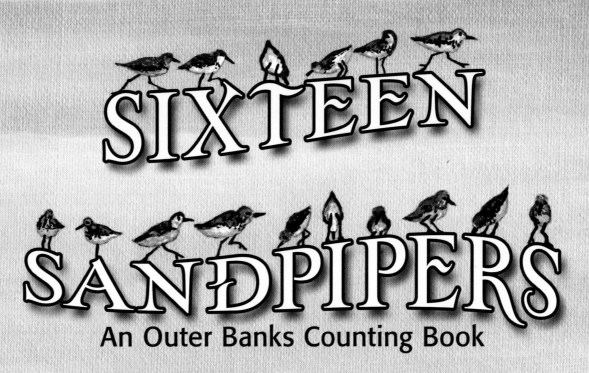

SIXTEEN SANDPIPERS

An Outer Banks Counting Book

WRITTEN BY
ANNE DAVIS CREEF

ILLUSTRATED BY
ASIA EVANS

Maritime Kids Quest Press

Published by Maritime Kids' Quest Press.

Library of Congress Control Number: 2009902783

ISBN 978-0-976-11787-2

CPSIA: Manufactured in the United States of America by BOOKMASTERS, Inc., 30 Amberwood Parkway, Ashland, OH, 44805; Job #M7457. Date of production: June 2010.

ACKNOWLEDGEMENTS

The author wishes to extend special thanks to her husband, Charlie Creef, who listened patiently as she read *Sixteen Sandpipers* at least one hundred times. Many thanks also to Claudia Fry S. Harrington for her guidance and help in making this book a reality.

To all my first grade students, past and present. This book was written for you.
— Anne Creef

To my loving parents, George and Michelle Evans, and to William.
— Asia Evans

1

ONE lighthouse with stripes black and white

2

TWO Wright brothers created the first flight

3 THREE sailors raise an old flag

4 FOUR silly otters play water tag

5

FIVE fluffy goslings
follow Mother Goose

6

SIX brown marsh bunnies
running loose

7 SEVEN young mallards keeping up with their flock

8 EIGHT colorful blue crabs hiding under a dock

9 NINE hungry nutria
nibble marsh grass

10 TEN silver mullets
jump high and splash

11
ELEVEN flowers in a garden by the sea

12 TWELVE red wolves
running wild and free

THIRTEEN lost colonists, and more. Where did they go?

14 FOURTEEN lazy pelicans glide along slow

15 FIFTEEN wild ponies guarding their turf

16 SIXTEEN sandpipers running from the surf

17 SEVENTEEN kites soar high above Jockey's Ridge

18 EIGHTEEN boats fish around Oregon Inlet Bridge

19 NINETEEN fishermen cast lines off Nags Head Pier

20 TWENTY snow geese arrive from far and near

21
TWENTY-ONE seagulls scream and squawk

23
TWENTY-THREE
cormorants black as night

24 TWENTY-FOUR dolphins diving out of sight

25 TWENTY-FIVE sea turtles hatch from their nest

26 TWENTY-SIX swans stop for a rest

27 TWENTY-SEVEN white ibis spread their wings wide

28

TWENTY-EIGHT jellyfish float in on the tide

29 TWENTY-NINE charter boats head back to shore
Full of happy fishermen and fishes galore!

30 THIRTY miles per hour the wind does blow,
Batten down the hatch and get below!

Sixteen Sandpipers Outer Banks Facts

1 The Cape Hatteras Lighthouse is the tallest lighthouse in the United States, 208 feet from base to beacon. Its distinctive black and white diagonal stripes and rotating light can be seen 20 miles offshore. For more than 100 years this lighthouse has warned ships away from the dangerous Diamond Shoals' sandbars. Other lighthouses along the Outer Banks are the Currituck Lighthouse, located in Corolla; the Bodie Island Lighthouse in South Nags Head; and the Ocracoke Lighthouse on Ocracoke Island.

2 In 1903, two intrepid young inventors, Orville and Wilber Wright, came to the Kitty Hawk area to experiment with their unique flying machine. On December 17th of that year, across the bare windswept dunes, the Wright brothers achieved the world's first successful passenger airplane flight. Today, the site is part of the Wright Brothers National Memorial, presented by the National Park Service. This beautiful park also includes historically reconstructed buildings, a visitors' center and museum, the Centennial Pavilion, and scenic walking/biking trails.

3 The *Elizabeth II*, a reproduction of a sixteenth century sailing ship, is similar to the vessel that transported the first settlers to Roanoke Island in 1585. Located on the Manteo waterfront, the ship is part of Roanoke Island Festival Park where visitors may enjoy guided tours of the ship led by sailors dressed in Elizabethan costumes.

4 The coastal marshes of the Outer Banks are home to North American river otters. These small, furry mammals are elusive and hard to spot in the wild, although clean-picked fish bones often provide evidence of their evening picnics on local docks. The North Carolina Aquarium on Roanoke Island is the best place to observe these appealing little creatures at play.

5 Each fall, thousands of Canada Geese migrate south to spend the winter along the Outer Banks'

shallow waterways. Hundreds of geese make this area their year round home. A dependable food supply and protected creeks create a perfect habitat for them to nest and raise a family.

6 Marsh rabbits are smaller, darker cousins of the common eastern cottontail rabbits. Unlike most rabbits, they are strong swimmers and are usually found close to water. Marsh rabbits do not live in burrows, but nest above ground in thickets or logs. Dawn and dusk are the best times for viewing them along the marshy roadsides as they feast upon grass and plants.

7 The bright green heads of the colorful male ducks, called drakes, make mallards easy to identify. Residents of salt marshes and creeks, they are plentiful along the Atlantic Coast.

8 Abundant in coastal waters, the blue crab is harvested by the thousands and is an important part of the Outer Banks seafood industry. "Going crabbing" has been a favorite summer activity of local children for decades. A long string with a chicken neck tied to the end is the perfect bait to lure a hard crab within swooping range of a dip net.

9 Nutria, often mistaken for muskrats, are semi-aquatic rodents with long round tails. Imported from South America for the fur trade, nutria have spread rapidly throughout southeastern coastal marshes and bays. They are vegetarians, voraciously consuming both water and land plants.

10 Mullets are silvery-gray fish common to the sounds and creeks of the Outer Banks. They are a favorite food of dolphins and other large fish. When chased by predators, schools of mullet will jump high from the water falling back with a splash.

11 Created in 1951, the Elizabethan Gardens on Roanoke Island are a lovely memorial to the first

English colonists. The gardens contain native flowers, trees, and shrubs, as well as exotic plants from around the globe. The Gardens' highlights include an ancient live oak tree, believed to be more than 400 years old; an exquisite marble statue of Virginia Dare, the first English child born in America; the world's largest bronze statue of HRH Queen Elizabeth I; and the Woodland & Wildlife children's garden.

12 The Alligator River National Wildlife refuge located on the Outer Banks mainland is home to a growing population of endangered red wolves. In the early 1970s the species was almost extinct. Thanks to the efforts of the U.S. Fish and Wildlife Service, red wolves again roam free in North Carolina.

13 *The Lost Colony*, written by Pulitzer Prize winner Paul Green, is the first and longest running outdoor drama in the United States. Presented at the historic Waterside Theatre on Roanoke Island, it tells the story of the mysterious disappearance of the first English colony in the New World. Traditionally, many of the roles in this exciting drama are played by actors native to the Outer Banks.

14 Once rarely seen along the Outer Banks, the stately brown pelican has made an almost miraculous comeback in recent years. Brown pelicans are excellent fishers, plunging headlong into the water and emerging with a bill full of fish.

15 Wild herds of small ponies once roamed free on Outer Banks beaches. However, urban growth and loss of habitat have reduced the ponies to just two small herds, one on Ocracoke Island and the other north of Corolla. Many legends surround the origin of the "banker" ponies, but most locals believe they are descendents of shipwrecked Spanish mustangs.

16 These busy little shorebirds, also known as Willets, spend their days chasing waves back and forth, probing the wet sand for tiny bits of food. Smaller than seagulls, sandpipers are an amusing sight as they dash within inches of the surf, retreating just in time to keep their tiny feet dry.

17 Jockey's Ridge is the largest natural sand dune on the East Coast. The dune, sometimes more than 140 feet high, continues to drift in a southwesterly direction, blown by a prevailing northeast wind off the Atlantic Ocean. The windy summit of Jockey's Ridge is a wonderful place to fly kites. On sunny days with clear blue skies, the kites create a swirling rainbow of shapes and colors — a truly spectacular sight!

18 Herbert C. Bonner Bridge, better known to locals as "Oregon Inlet Bridge", spans beautiful Oregon Inlet, one of the best fishing spots on the East Coast, located on the southern end of Bodie Island. Created in 1946 by a powerful hurricane, the inlet was named after the *Oregon*, the first vessel to pass through. On calm sunny days, Oregon Inlet is usually filled with small boats. On rough windy days, only the bigger charter boats venture through its treacherous waters.

19 You don't need a boat to catch fish on the Outer Banks. Numerous fishing piers from Kitty Hawk to Frisco attract anglers in all kinds of weather. Lucky fishermen may hook anything from small sea mullet to giant cobia.

20 Pea Island National Refuge on the north end of Hatteras Island attracts thousands of migratory waterfowl during the spring and fall. Flocks of snow geese begin arriving in late fall to feast on the wild dune peas that give Pea Island its name. Nature trails and viewing platforms allow visitors to observe more than 300 species of birds.

21 Seagulls in shades of brown, black, gray and white are seen everywhere along the Outer Banks. No day on the beach is complete without the background sounds of squabbling gulls. They are strong fliers and wily scavengers. Seagulls are often seen circling fishing and crab boats hoping for a tasty tidbit.

22 Minnows are baby fish. They are found in all colors and shapes depending on the species. Minnows swim in every body of water on the Outer Banks, from the Atlantic Ocean to shallow tidal pools, creeks, ponds, and ditches. These quick little fish provide food for birds, small mammals, and larger fish.

23 Cormorants are large, dark sea birds with hooked bills. They dive from the surface and swim rapidly underwater to catch fish. At sunset, flocks of cormorants make beautiful silhouettes as they skim across the waters of the Outer Banks.

24 The waters of Roanoke Sound, Croatan Sound, and Pamlico Sound are home to numerous pods of dolphins in the summer and early fall. Food is plentiful and the shallow waterways provide a safe place to raise their offspring. Young dolphins are often seen playfully riding in the wake behind boats and even bodysurfing in the ocean breakers.

25 The sandy beaches of the Outer Banks provide a nesting area for several species of endangered sea turtles. Female turtles crawl up onto the beach at night and dig nests in the sand, depositing between 75 and 200 eggs. Each female covers her nest with sand then returns to the sea. In about two months, usually at night, the eggs hatch and the tiny turtles scurry toward the ocean to begin their fight for survival.

26 Each year thousands of migrating Tundra Swans winter along the sounds, ponds, and tidal flats of the Outer Banks. The large white, graceful birds are easily recognized. At rest, the swans appear to be a sea of white feathers floating gently on the dark winter water.

27 With their long curved reddish-orange bills, tall thin legs, and bright white feathers, ibis are unique wading birds. They can be found during the day in marshes, ditches, and shallow ponds, probing the mud for a meal. When dusk arrives, ibis roost in large flocks in shrubs and trees.

28 Jellyfish are common in the ocean and sound waters that surround the Outer Banks. Although most are beautiful, with graceful bodies and colorful tentacles, many species of jellyfish contain poisonous stinging cells. It's best to stay away from them!

29 Charter fishing along the Outer Banks is excellent. During the spring, summer and early fall, large numbers of charter boats leave local marinas daily for inshore and offshore fishing trips. For generations, Outer Banks natives have made it a tradition to go down to the docks in the late afternoon to view the day's catch.

30 Constant wind is a fact of Outer Banks life. Locals who make their living from the sea keep a close eye on the weather. Fishermen listen to marine weather forecasts before venturing out to sea, but also keep a close eye on the sky and water at all times. Weather lore has been passed from older generations to younger sailors, and every boat captain knows to pay attention to the saying, "red sky in the morning, sailors take warning".

• • • • • • •

31

THIRTY-ONE DAYS may be just enough time to explore the Outer Banks and enjoy the bright sunshine!

Author Anne Davis Creef is a native of Roanoke Island, on the Outer Banks of North Carolina. Her family history dates back on both sides to the late 1700s, the beginnings of permanent English settlement along the Outer Banks. Mrs. Creef's Etheridge and Dough grandfathers proudly served in the United States Lifesaving Service long before it was re-established as the United States Coast Guard in 1915. Her great-grandfather, Willie Dough, was present at the Wright brothers' first flight, December 17, 1903. Mrs. Creef's grandfathers from her Creef lineage were accomplished boat builders who designed the shad boat, which is now the North Carolina state boat.

Anne has been teaching for nearly twenty-five years and currently teaches at Manteo Elementary School on Roanoke Island. As a child, she loved exploring the sounds, creeks, and wetlands that surround the island. Mrs. Creef wrote this book with the hope that children everywhere would enjoy learning about the unique history and beauty of the windswept Outer Banks of North Carolina.

Illustrator Stella Asia Evans is also a native of Roanoke Island, with family history on the Outer Banks dating back to the late 1700s. Asia was introduced to art at an early age by her father, George Hunter Evans, who was her first art teacher and a huge influence on her painting style.

Ms. Evans graduated with an Associate's Degree in Fine Arts from the College of the Albemarle's Dare Campus. She also holds an Associate of Applied Science Degree in Interior Design from the Art Institute of Charlotte where she was selected by her professors to receive the Award for Most Outstanding Interior Design Student.

Asia is currently applying her education as an interior designer for Kellogg Design Center in Manteo and Nags Head. She feels quite fortunate to have grown up on the Outer Banks as the area has always been her inspiration and truly the only place she could call home.

Ms. Evans continues to enjoy painting, especially of Outer Banks wildlife.